Dolphins are friendly, playful, and intelligent animals. They are often seen swimming around boats and jumping in and out of the waves. They live in families called pods.

There are about forty different types of dolphins. They range in size from male orcas, which are about 9m long, down to Hector's dolphins, which are about 1.5m long.

Many dolphins are endangered due to hunting. They also sadly become trapped in fishing nets and plastic litter.

Dolphins have long snouts with cone-shaped teeth, and eyes on the sides of their heads. Dolphins talk to each other using whistles, clicks, squawks, and yelps.

They live in seas or rivers, and have fins and a tail like a fish, but they are actually mammals. A dolphin breathes air using the blowhole on the top of its head.

As they are mammals, dolphins give birth to live young. The baby dolphins are often born tail-first, and they can see, hear, and swim from birth.

As soon as they are born, they are helped to the surface to take their first breaths.

Dolphins normally have one baby at a time. The baby dolphin drinks milk from its mother. The mother and baby stay together for a long time, sometimes up to six years.

The young dolphins swim in the middle of the pod to keep them safe from predators, such as sharks and orcas.

The most common sort of dolphin is the bottlenose dolphin. They are found everywhere except in the Arctic and Antarctic circles.

Bottlenose dolphins are about 4m long and are so dark that sometimes they look black.

bottlenose dolphin

Dolphins can live for up to 40 (forty) years and some have been known to reach 60 (sixty) years of age.

Hector's dolphins are the smallest type of dolphin. They have black and white markings. They have a black stripe that runs from their face to their flippers. They eat fish and squid.

Hector's dolphin

Hector's dolphins live in small pods. They are only found around the coast of New Zealand. There is a very small number of them left.

Orcas are often called killer whales, but they are actually a type of dolphin and not a whale at all!

Their teeth are cone-shaped.

They have distinctive black and white markings. Individual orcas can be identified by looking at the different shapes and patches on them.

Orcas are normally between 5m and 8m long. They hunt in pods for fish, seals, seabirds, turtles, and other sea mammals such as walruses.

Orcas sometimes force other animals, such as seals or walruses, onto land to catch them. They have been seen throwing seals up into the air and then hitting them with their tails to stun them.

Here are some other sorts of dolphins that have "whale" in their name:

the melon-headed whale

the pygmy killer whale

the false killer whale

the short-finned pilot whale

Long-finned pilot whales are the second largest type of dolphin, at 4m to 6m long, and they do indeed have very long pectoral fins! They feed at night in very deep parts of the sea.

long-finned pilot whale

Long ago, people used to think that each pod was led or "piloted" by one animal. This is not true, but the animals in the pods do stay together and help each other. Pilot whales can end up stranded because they sometimes swim onto beaches and then cannot get back to the sea.

Dolphins' intelligence can be useful to humans. Some dolphins have found ways to help people hunt fish.

Sometimes, hunting dolphins produce bubbles to herd fish to the surface. They blow bubbles while swimming in a circle. The bubbles float up and form a sort of net. This confuses the fish and makes them swim closer together, making it easier for the dolphins to catch them.

Bottlenose dolphins also hunt by fish whacking. They hit the fish with their tails to stun them, and then they swim along and eat the stunned fish.

a bait ball of sardines

Sometimes, a pod of dolphins will herd a shoal of fish into a smaller and smaller ball called a bait ball. The dolphins then swim up from underneath, into the tightly-packed ball of fish, and eat as many as they can.

Some dolphins only live in rivers, and do not go out to sea at all. They have less blubber (fat) because it is not as cold in rivers as it is in the sea.

a river dolphin

The Ganges and Indus river dolphins are blind. They send out sound waves to navigate, find food, and talk with each other.

River dolphins are endangered because many rivers are polluted.

The rarest type of dolphin often found in rivers is the Irawaddy (pronounced "Ira-woddy"). They have a rounded face and a short snout. They often become tangled up in fishing nets and drown.

In Myanmar, Irawaddy dolphins are known to help local fishermen.

The fishermen bang on the sides of their boats to call the dolphins. The dolphins then help the fishermen by herding fish into their nets.

Scientists have discovered that dolphins evolved from animals that once lived on land and walked on four legs. They can tell this by looking at fossils. About 50,000,000 (fifty million) years ago, the dolphins' ancestors went back into the sea. Gradually, their back legs became a tail and their forelegs became flippers.

This is also why dolphins' tails go up and down when they swim and not side to side as fish tails do.